GREAT PRAYERS
OF THE BIBLE

12 Studies for Individuals or Groups

CAROL PLUEDDEMANN

Harold Shaw Publishers • Wheaton, Illinois

ISBN 0-87788-334-3

Cover photo by © 1994 by Mark Doebler

99   98   97   96   95   94

10   9   8   7   6   5   4   3

CONTENTS

INTRODUCTION

This is a study of twelve specific prayers in Scripture. As you study these, you will have the opportunity to listen in on some of the most significant prayers in human history. You will gain new insights about prayer and how to pray, but you'll also learn about the people who voiced these prayers and the God to whom they prayed.

You will find that the circumstances that drove these people to prayer reflect your own concerns. The heart-cries of these prayers will echo your own deepest questions.

By studying the prayers of Scripture, you will be impressed that prayer is a privilege open to everyone. There is no priestly monopoly on prayer. Though some prayers are literary and poetic, others are simple and spontaneous. All of them fill us with the wonder of communicating with our Creator.

These prayers are only a sample of the many prayers in Scripture. You will want to study others on your own and make them a part of your life. Your prayers will be enriched as you make these great prayers of Scripture models for your own interaction with God.

HOW TO USE THIS STUDYGUIDE

Fisherman studyguides are based on the inductive approach to Bible study. Inductive study is discovery study; we discover what the Bible says as we ask questions about its content and search for answers. This is quite different from the process in which a teacher *tells* a group *about* the Bible and what it means and what to do about it. In inductive study God speaks directly to each of us through his Word.

A group functions best when a leader keeps the discussion on target, but this leader is neither the teacher nor the "answer person." A leader's responsibility is to *ask*—not *tell*. The answers come from the text itself as group members examine, discuss, and think together about the passage.

There are four kinds of questions in each study. The first is an *approach question*. Used before the Bible passage is read, this question breaks the ice and helps you focus on the topic of the Bible study. It begins to reveal where thoughts and feelings need to be transformed by Scripture.

Some of the earlier questions in each study are *observation questions* designed to help you find out basic facts—who, what, where, when, and how.

When you know what the Bible says you need to ask, *What does it mean?* These *interpretation questions* help you to discover the writer's basic message.

Application questions ask, *What does it mean to me?* They challenge you to live out the Scripture's life-transforming message.

Fisherman studyguides provide spaces between questions for jotting down responses and related questions you would like to raise in the group. Each group member should have a copy of the studyguide and may take a turn in leading the group.

A group should use any accurate, modern translation of the Bible such as the *New International Version,* the *New American Standard Bible,* the *Revised Standard Version,* the *New Jerusalem Bible,* or the *Good News Bible.* (Other translations or paraphrases of the Bible may be referred to when additional help is needed.) Bible commentaries should not be brought to a Bible study because they tend to dampen discussion and keep people from thinking for themselves.

SUGGESTIONS FOR GROUP LEADERS

1. Read and study the Bible passage thoroughly beforehand, grasping its themes and applying its teachings for yourself. Pray that the Holy Spirit will "guide you into truth" so that your leadership will guide others.

2. If the studyguide's questions ever seem ambiguous or unnatural to you, rephrase them, feeling free to add others that seem necessary to bring out the meaning of a verse.

3. Begin (and end) the study promptly. Start by asking someone to pray for God's help. Remember, the Holy Spirit is the teacher, not you!

4. Ask for volunteers to read the passages out loud.

5. As you ask the studyguide's questions in sequence, encourage everyone to participate in the discussion. If some are silent, ask, "What do you think, Heather?" or, "Dan, what can you add to that answer?" or suggest, "Let's have an answer from someone who hasn't spoken up yet."

6. If a question comes up that you can't answer, don't be afraid to admit that you're baffled! Assign the topic as a research project for someone to report on next week.

7. Keep the discussion moving and focused. Though tangents will inevitably be introduced, you can bring the discussion back to the topic at hand. Learn to pace the discussion so that you finish a study each session you meet.

8. Don't be afraid of silences: some questions take time to answer and some people need time to gather courage to speak. If silence persists, rephrase your question, but resist the temptation to answer it yourself.

9. If someone comes up with an answer that is clearly illogical or unbiblical, ask him or her for further clarification: "What verse suggests that to you?"

10. Discourage Bible-hopping and overuse of cross-references. Learn all you can from *this* passage, along with a few important references suggested in the studyguide.

11. Some questions are marked with a ♦. This indicates that further information is available in the Leader's Notes at the back of the guide.

12. For further information on getting a new Bible study group started and keeping it functioning effectively, read Gladys Hunt's *You Can Start a Bible Study Group* and *Pilgrims in Progress: Growing through Groups* by Jim and Carol Plueddemann.

SUGGESTIONS FOR GROUP MEMBERS

1. Learn and apply the following ground rules for effective Bible study. (If new members join the group later, review these guidelines with the whole group.)

2. Remember that your goal is to learn all that you can *from the Bible passage being studied.* Let it speak for itself without using Bible commentaries or other Bible passages. There is more than enough in each assigned passage to keep your group productively occupied for one session. Sticking to the passage saves the group from insecurity and confusion.

3. Avoid the temptation to bring up those fascinating tangents that don't really grow out of the passage you are discussing. If the topic is of common interest, you can bring it up later in informal conversation following the study. Meanwhile, help each other stick to the subject!

4. Encourage each other to participate. People remember best what they discover and verbalize for themselves. Some people are naturally shyer than others, or they may be afraid of making a mistake. If your discussion is free and friendly and you show real interest in what other group members think and feel, they will be more likely to speak up. Remember, the more people involved in a discussion, the richer it will be.

5. Guard yourself from answering too many questions or talking too much. Give others a chance to express themselves. If you are one who participates easily, discipline yourself by counting to ten before you open your mouth!

6. Make personal, honest applications and commit yourself to letting God's Word change you.

ABRAHAM
What Is God Like?

Genesis 18:1-33

My husband is a college prof, and it's interesting to watch the interaction that takes place between him and his students. At the beginning of the year, students wonder what this prof is like. They tend to be intimidated and a bit cautious because of their stereotypical ideas about professors. All of that soon changes as they get to know what Jim is really like. They realize that he sees them as peers, friends, and colleagues. They can talk to him about anything—as long as it's not past his ten o'clock bedtime!

We approach someone according to what we think he or she is like. Sometimes, weeks or months down the line, we realize that our approach hasn't really matched the person; we discover that the rejection, the harsh judgment of our character, or the indifference we expected are simply nonexistent. And we're relieved to find in their place acceptance, laughter, and love.

What is God like? And what can we ask of God? These questions are at the heart of our prayer concerns. They were Abraham's questions, too.

♦ **1.** Describe a time when you wanted to question God about something that didn't make sense to you. Were you able to express your concerns to him?

Read Genesis 18:1-15.

♦ **2.** When do you think Abraham begins to suspect the identity of his visitors?

Note: One of the visitors represents God revealed in the flesh and is referred to as "the Lord." The other two "men" are later described as angelic beings (19:1).

Read Genesis 18:16-33.

3. How does it strike you to "overhear" God's thoughts in verses 17-19?

4. Why should God bother to tell Abraham his intentions?

5. What difference should it make to our praying to know that God shares his thoughts and plans with us?

♦ **6.** What concerns cause Abraham to pray so intensely?

♦ **7.** What is Abraham really asking God (verse 25)?

8. What different emotions does Abraham experience as he prays?

◆ **9.** Why do you think Abraham stops at ten in his request?

10. What impresses you about this conversation between God and Abraham?

11. What does Abraham learn about God through this dialogue?

♦ **12.** For whom is God calling you to intercede? How does Abraham's example encourage you? Spend some time now praying together for those God has brought to your mind.

HANNAH
A Cry and a Song

1 Samuel 1:1-20; 2:1-10

Several years ago, a couple in our Bible study asked the group to pray with them about their desire to have a child. Week after week, month after month, we interceded with God on their behalf. We were elated when they happily announced they were expecting, but then grieved with them when the pregnancy ended in a miscarriage. It was a faith-testing time for all of us, and we continued to pray. Eventually, a healthy baby was conceived and delivered. We all rejoiced over this gift of life that was given in answer to persevering prayer.

Hannah's childless despair was symptomatic of the larger wretched-ness that Israel was experiencing during the barren days of the judges. The miracle answer to her prayers was also an answer from God to Israel's distress. Samuel fulfilled Hannah's longings for a child and grew up to lead Israel faithfully through the last era of the judges and into the new kingship.

1. How do you respond when God seems to be saying "no" to your prayers?

Read 1 Samuel 1:1-20.

♦ **2.** The books of 1 and 2 Samuel tell the story of Israel's great history. What, do you think, is the significance of beginning the narrative with this simple and touching account?

♦ **3.** Why might God have allowed Hannah to come to such a pitch of desperation?

4. What do you think Hannah prayed in her heart as "her lips were moving"?

5. Notice the change that took place in Hannah's outlook between verses 7 and 18. What caused her sadness to disappear?

Read 1 Samuel 2:1-10.

◆ **6.** Hannah's prayer song has been called the "Magnificat of the Old Testament" because it is so similar to Mary's Magnificat in the New Testament (Luke 1:46-55). Who is the supreme source of Hannah's joy?

7. What do you learn in this prayer of praise about the God Hannah worships?

◆ **8.** What surprising reversals does Hannah describe?

◆ **9.** Hannah's prayer also describes the experience of Israel as a nation. What examples of this parallel do you see?

10. In what circumstances are you tempted to trust in your own strength (verse 9)? What could help you to trust more in God's strength?

♦ **11.** How can Hannah's example encourage you when you face "barrenness" in your life?

12. Pray your longings to God now—as a cry or a song.

DAVID
A Prayer at the End of Life

1 Chronicles 29:1-30

When preparing tax returns for our recently deceased father, we were astounded to see the percentage of his income that he gave to God's work. His giving pattern made a strong statement to us about what really matters in life. This spiritual legacy blessed us and challenged us to give more of ourselves to God.

As David came to the end of his life, he gave his whole fortune for the building of the temple. This in turn encouraged all the people to give freely and wholeheartedly to the Lord. David's prayer of dedication expresses his praise to God and his concerns for his people.

♦ **1.** What models of giving influenced you when you were growing up?

Read 1 Chronicles 29:1-9.

◆   **2.** What principles of giving do you see in these verses?

Read 1 Chronicles 29:10-30.

3. What do verses 10-16 reveal about David's view of God? His view of people?

4. How does David's view of God influence his giving?

5. What further principles of giving do you see in verses 17-19?

6. What were David's concerns for the people and his son Solomon?

7. If you were nearing the end of your life, what concerns would you want to express in prayer for your family and friends?

♦ **8.** In what different ways did David and his people express their devotion to God (verses 6-22)?

9. Solomon could have had mixed feelings about his inheritance being given for the temple. How is his reign described in verse 25? Again, who is acknowledged as the source and controller of prosperity?

10. How might David's prayer influence your plans for the way you will invest your life?

11. What steps could you take now to ensure that you will leave a spiritual legacy to your loved ones? Pray together for wisdom and courage to take these steps.

SOLOMON
"Hear and Forgive"

2 Chronicles 6:1–7:4

A newspaper article reporting on a civic ceremony said, "The distinguished Reverend Doctor Archibald Fitzsimmons directed a beautiful prayer to those assembled."

That's the problem with many public prayers—they're directed to people rather than to God. But God isn't swayed by impressive words and pious phrases. He is concerned with the condition of the heart. Solomon's prayer emphasizes the need for confession and forgiveness—a good model for private and public prayer.

1. In your experience, what are the benefits and the drawbacks of public prayer?

Read 2 Chronicles 6:1-11.

2. Notice all the references to the *Name of the Lord*. How do these underscore the purpose for the temple?

Read 2 Chronicles 6:12-21.

◆ **3.** What does Solomon express by his body language (verses 12-13)?

4. What does Solomon affirm about God as he begins his prayer?

◆ **5.** How does Solomon answer his own question in verse 18?

6. List all the different expressions Solomon uses in verses 19-21 to appeal to God. Why might he approach God this way?

♦ **7.** What false ideas might people have about the temple? Why then would Solomon encourage praying toward the temple?

Read 2 Chronicles 6:22-42.

♦ **8.** Solomon describes seven different situations when the people would need God's help. What common elements do you find in each of these situations? (Each one is introduced by the word *when.*)

♦ **9.** What different actions does Solomon ask God to take in these verses?

10. What do you learn about repentance and forgiveness in this passage?

11. What similar needs do we have today that call for God to "hear us and forgive"?

Read 2 Chronicles 7:1-4.

12. How did God respond to Solomon's prayer? How did the people respond?

♦ **13.** Solomon refers to many of God's characteristics in his prayer. Which of these is most important to you when you approach God in prayer? Praise him for that characteristic now as you pray together.

JOB
Trusting God for Who He Is

Job 38:1-18; 40:1-5; 42:1-16

"Why, God?" Who hasn't prayed these words? If anyone ever had cause to ask God "why?" it was Job. He was "blameless and upright," yet he was deluged with tragedy—the death of his children, the loss of all his possessions, and an agonizing illness. Satan himself was trying to drive a wedge between Job and God, yet Job was mostly unaware of this larger drama.

Throughout the book, Job and his friends debate his case. Job longs to meet God so he can argue his innocence before him personally (23:3-5). Now God finally speaks, and this is where our study of Job's prayer begins. We can only look at parts of the conversation between Job and God, but you will want to read the whole prayer in chapters 38–42 on your own.

1. Describe a time when you felt small or were "brought down to size."

Read Job 38:1-18.

2. Job has been looking for answers to his questions about human suffering. What does God do instead of providing answers?

3. Why do you think God chooses this approach to Job?

4. What phrases do you find particularly striking in this poetic passage?

◆ **5.** What picture of God emerges from these questions? How does this compare with the picture you have of God?

6. What does this passage say about human nature in general? About Job?

Read Job 40:1-5.

◆ **7.** How does Job respond to God?

8. According to verse 2, who is really on trial here?

9. What brings Job to this point of recognizing his own insignificance before God?

Read Job 42:1-6.

10. What does Job understand now that he didn't before? What is his response to this new understanding?

11. Chapter 1 explains that Job's suffering was part of a larger battle between God and Satan, but there is no indication that Job was aware of that. What difference does it make to you to know that you participate in the heavenly battle between good and evil?

12. What new insights does Job's conversation with God give you about the place of suffering in your own life?

Read the epilogue of Job's life in Job 42:7-16.

◆ **13.** What part did prayer have in Job's restoration?

14. How can Job's prayer serve as an example to you when you are tested? Pray together now for godly responses to trials group members are facing.

DANIEL
A Scriptural Agenda
for Prayer

Daniel 9:1-19

What worries keep you awake at night? What questions burn in your mind? What concerns consume your energy? Often we trick ourselves into thinking that we're devoted to the right priorities, to God's agenda. But when we stop to analyze our thoughts and activities, a different picture emerges. And what about our prayers? Do they reflect God's concerns for the world?

1. Think honestly about the content of your most recent prayers. What concerns are reflected in your prayers?

Read Daniel 9:1-19.

◆ **2.** How did Daniel become aware of his need to pray?

3. Jeremiah had prophesied that Jerusalem would be desolate for seventy years. The seventy years were now accomplished, but nothing had changed. How did Daniel respond to this situation? How might he have responded differently?

4. How does Daniel begin his prayer (verse 4)?

5. In what ways had the people sinned?

6. Notice Daniel's preoccupation with God's character. What contrasts do these verses point out between God and the people of Israel?

7. On what basis does Daniel plead with God (verse 18)?

8. To which of God's concerns does Daniel appeal? How does this add boldness to his prayer?

♦ **9.** Note the various uses of Scripture in the whole passage. Does your study of Scripture prompt you to pray as Daniel did? How could you make Scripture an integral element of your prayers?

10. Think back to question 1. What concerns do you want to make the focus of your life? How can your prayers reflect those concerns more faithfully?

◆ **11.** How can you be more actively concerned about the honor and reputation of God among people around you?

◆ **12.** Spend some time in prayer as a group, praying according to Daniel's agenda in this passage.

HABAKKUK
Praying with God's Perspective

Habakkuk 3:1-19

The whole book of Habakkuk is actually a prayer—a conversation between Habakkuk and God. In the first two chapters, Habakkuk argues with God over his incomprehensible ways. He complains that evil is going unpunished in Judah, and God doesn't seem to be doing anything about it. God replies that he will punish Judah through the Babylonians. Hearing God say that he will use the ruthless, godless Babylonians to punish people more righteous than they only adds to Habakkuk's perplexity. God assures Habakkuk that eventually Babylon itself will be destroyed and faith will be rewarded. After receiving God's replies, Habakkuk responds with a great prayer of faith.

1. Describe a time when you echoed Habakkuk's words, "How long, O Lord, must I call for help, but you do not listen?" (Habakkuk 1:2).

Read Habakkuk 3:1-19.

♦ **2.** Habakkuk stands in awe of God's deeds (verse 2). To what events in Israel's history might verses 3-15 refer?

Note: Habakkuk's personal struggle to understand God's ways also represented Judah's struggle. This prayer became a public expression of Israel's faith. The words shigionoth *(verse 1) and* selah *(verses 3, 9, 13) are probably musical or liturgical terms.*

3. How does this recitation of God's marvelous deeds help Habakkuk anticipate deliverance in his day (verse 2)?

4. How might God's wrath and God's mercy be related (verse 2)?

5. How do the images in verses 3-15 inspire awe and worship in you?

6. What was Habakkuk's response to this dramatic vision (verse 16)?

7. What merciful and mighty deeds has God done in your past that you would like him to renew in your present situation?

♦ **8.** Look closely at Habakkuk's affirmation in verses 17-18. Why would it be difficult for Habakkuk to pray these words?

9. In the midst of great fear, who is the focus of Habakkuk's joy (verses 18-19)? What gives Habakkuk such sure-footed confidence?

♦ **10.** In your life, what are your greatest fears for the future? Substitute these fears for the disasters Habakkuk lists. Can you affirm Habakkuk's words in verse 18—even if your worst fear materializes? Use Habakkuk's prayer as a model to pray about your fears and to affirm your faithfulness to God.

THE LEVITES
A Prayer of Corporate Confession

Nehemiah 9:1-38

The usual pattern of fasting before feasting is changed in Nehemiah 8 and 9. Chapter 8 describes a celebration feast of great joy that lasted seven days. Each day during that feast, Ezra, the scribe, read from the Book of the Law of God (8:18). Then on the twenty-fourth day of the month, the people began a time of fasting. They covered themselves with sackcloth and sprinkled dust on their heads. It seems clear that the Word they heard during the feast convicted them of their true condition. The result was humble confession.

1. When you were growing up, what did "confession" mean to you?

Read Nehemiah 9:1-5.

2. How did the Israelites prepare for their time of confession?

Read Nehemiah 9:6-25.

◆ **3.** Make a note of the major turning points in Israel's history recorded in these verses. How was God's grace and power demonstrated in each one?

◆ **4.** In what ways would this prayer have given a sense of identity to the Jewish people? Why would this be important at this particular time in their history?

Read Nehemiah 9:26-31.

5. What pattern do you see in this prayer of the relationship between God and his people?

6. How does this pattern compare with the relationship you have with God?

7. What did God use to bring his people back to himself?

8. What has God used in your life to bring you back to himself or to keep you close to him? How have you responded?

9. Do your blessings increase your thankfulness to God or do they tend to make you feel independent of God?

Read Nehemiah 9:32-38.

♦ **10.** How did the people feel about God's treatment of them? What did they see as the source of their problems?

11. How does this prayer show a balance between pride and shame, regret and thankfulness?

12. What have been the major "turning points" in your personal history?

What signposts of God's grace and power have you seen?

13. In view of God's faithfulness, what renewed commitment do you want to make for your present situation? As you pray together, thank God for his active involvement in your lives, and pray for renewed obedience to follow him wholeheartedly.

MARY
A Prayer of Joy

Luke 1:26-56

Mary has often been portrayed as a sorrowful woman. She experienced deep grief as Jesus' mother, culminating in the agony of watching his crucifixion. But Mary is also called blessed. William Barclay comments, "Nowhere can we better see the paradox of blessedness than in the life of Mary. To Mary was granted the blessedness of being the mother of the Son of God. Well might her heart be filled with a wondering, tremulous, amazed joy at so great a privilege. And yet that very blessedness meant that some day she would see that Son of hers hanging on the cross. To be chosen by God so often means at one and the same time a crown of joy and a cross of sorrow" *(The Gospel of Luke: The Daily Study Bible,* p. 8). Mary's prayer is a beautiful response of submission to God's plan for her.

1. When have you experienced the seeming paradox of fearful belief, or doubting trust?

Read Luke 1:26-38.

2. Notice the precise details of *who, what, when,* and *where* in verses 26 and 27 that establish the setting for this event.

♦ **3.** What does Mary learn about herself from the angel? What does she learn about her coming child?

♦ **4.** What appears to be impossible about this announcement? And what makes it possible?

5. How might the news of Elizabeth's pregnancy encourage Mary?

6. Contrast Mary's responses in verses 34 and 38. Imagine the emotions she experiences. How does Mary's response encourage you?

Read Luke 1:39-45.

7. What is Elizabeth's reaction to Mary? How might this make Mary feel?

Read Luke 1:46-56.

♦ **8.** What does Mary express about her relationship to God in this prayer song?

9. What does Mary's prayer say about God's character? His actions? His attitude toward people?

10. How would Jesus fulfill the themes of Mary's prayer?

11. Mary's prayer shows God as one who is concerned for justice, mercy, and deliverance. How does your life reflect these concerns?

12. As you pray together, put your immediate problems in the perspective of God's past and future faithfulness as Mary does. Pray for the grace to submit joyfully to God's will as shown in Mary's response to the difficult role God gave her.

JESUS
A Prayer for His Family

Matthew 6:5-15

We have learned from the prayers of great people of faith such as
Abraham, Hannah, David, and Mary. Now we have the privilege of
learning to pray from Jesus himself.

Jesus' prayer is the simplest of prayers and the most complex of
prayers. It has just six petitions, but praying these with sincerity
demands supernatural help.

1. Which rote prayers were you taught as a child? Were
these helpful to you or not?

Read Matthew 6:5-15.

♦ **2.** According to verses 5-8, what is the wrong way to pray? The right way?

3. Make a list of all that you can know about God in this passage (including verses 5-8).

♦ **4.** On what relationship is true prayer based?

♦ **5.** What does it mean to you that Jesus instructed us to address God as "Father"?

♦ **6.** What does the designation "Our Father" imply about our relationship to other believers?

7. What kind of relationship to other people does God intend for us to have? (Look at the whole passage.)

♦ **8.** What does it mean to hallow God's name?

9. Notice the order of this prayer. Why does praying for God's kingdom fit appropriately after verse 9?

10. Look back to the characteristics of God you found in question 3. What would it mean to pray "your will be done" to this kind of God?

◆ **11.** In what ways does this prayer cover all of life?

◆ **12.** What is the relationship between forgiveness and prayer?

13. Using Jesus' prayer as an outline, pray together now for the specific needs of your group.

JESUS
A Farewell Prayer

John 17

We know that Jesus prayed often to his Father. But what were those conversations like? Here is one of Jesus' prayers that we can follow in detail. And what joy to "eavesdrop" on this prayer and discover Jesus praying for *us!* It's all the more wonderful when we remember that this was Jesus' last evening with his disciples before his arrest and death. At this agonizing hour, his prayers focused on those he loved and on those who would become part of his family in the future.

1. How do you handle "good-byes" in your family?

Read John 17:1-5.

♦ **2.** Chapters 13–16 record Jesus' final instructions to his disciples. Now he looks toward heaven and prays. First he prays for himself. Why does he want the Father to glorify him?

3. What was the work Jesus had completed (verse 4)?

Read John 17:6-19.

4. What are Jesus' requests for his disciples?

5. If Jesus had prayed only for the urgent short-term needs his disciples would face, how would this prayer be different?

♦ **6.** Circle each use of the word *world*. How does Jesus view the world?

7. What do you notice about the way that Jesus, his Father, and the disciples relate to each other? How could this relationship help the disciples in their mission to the world?

8. Three times Jesus spoke of protection for his disciples. What kind of protection would they need?

Read John 17:20-26.

◆ **9.** For whom does Jesus pray now? What is his concern for them?

10. Why does Jesus pray for unity among future believers?

11. What kind of unity exists between Jesus and the Father? How does your union with God through Christ affect your relationships with other believers? How else should it?

12. Do your prayers tend to reflect short-term, urgent needs, or long-term, eternal needs? As you pray for each other now, ask the Father for those requests Jesus prayed for.

PAUL
Bold Prayer for
Ultimate Concerns

Ephesians 3:14-21

My father used to comment that the majority of prayers seem to focus on stomachs or fenders! We pray for the sick and for safety in travel—good subjects for prayer, but should these be our priority?

Paul's prayers focused on the spiritual health of those he loved. He was concerned about the ultimate goal of life, and his prayers reflected that concern.

1. When have you felt strong in your Christian life? What were the contributing factors to this strength?

Paul begins chapter 3 with the intention of recording his prayer for the Ephesians, but then pauses to describe the "mystery of Christ." He explains it in verse 6: "This mystery is that through the gospel the Gentiles are heirs together with Israel, members together of one body, and sharers together in the promise in Christ Jesus."

Read Ephesians 3:14-19.

♦ **2.** Paul resumes the statement he began in verse 1: "For this reason . . ." Look back to Ephesians 2:19-22 and 3:6. What is the reason for Paul's prayer?

3. The ordinary position for prayer among the Jews was to stand with outstretched hands, palms upward. What might Paul's kneeling position indicate about his attitude in this prayer?

♦ **4.** To whom does Paul address his prayer? What con
fidence would verse 15 give to the Gentile believers?

5. List Paul's requests for the Ephesians. What themes
stand out?

6. Note the references to the three persons of the Trinity
in these verses. What do you learn about their roles?

♦ **7.** How can we know something that surpasses knowledge (verse 19)? What do you think Paul meant?

♦ **8.** Paul was aware of the danger of a faith that depended simply on intellectual knowledge. How does his prayer reflect that concern?

9. In whose company does a person come to understand the love of Christ (verse 18)? What implications do you see in this?

10. How does Paul emphasize the extent of Christ's love?

Read John 17:20-21.

♦ **11.** How does Paul's intercession lead naturally to praise?

12. In what ways is God's glory to be seen? For how long?

13. Who are the people in your life for whom you are most concerned? Use Paul's prayer to help you focus on the eternal, ultimate needs of those for whom you pray. Then close your prayer time and these studies with the doxology in verses 20-21.

LEADER'S NOTES

Question 1. Each study will begin with an approach question to help group members begin to think about the theme as it relates to their lives. Ask this question before reading the Scripture passage and allow several minutes for group response.

Question 2. Don't spend too much time on this first Scripture passage. It provides background for understanding the prayer in Genesis 18:23-33.

It's hard to know when Abraham and Sarah first realized that one of the strangers was the Lord. We don't know if they conversed during the meal or if Abraham had mentioned Sarah's name. If he hadn't, it would be quite startling to hear his guests ask where Sarah was and to hear one of them predict the birth of a son.

Question 6. Abraham was not only concerned for Lot, or he would not have stopped short of asking God to spare the city for the sake of ten righteous people. He must have been concerned about other people in Sodom as well as his own family.

Question 7. "It is not the fate of Sodom that is the issue in Abraham's prayer, but the character of God. It is easy enough to plead for the doomed and the lost, but it is another matter altogether to question God about his own integrity" (John White, *Daring to Draw Near,* p. 20. Downers Grove, Ill.: InterVarsity Press, 1977).

Question 9. Abraham is reassured and satisfied by God's responses. Whether Sodom is destroyed or not, he can trust God's character.

Question 12. Since this is a studyguide on prayer, it is important for your group to take time to pray together, applying what you learn from the great prayers in Scripture. Each study will suggest a focus for your prayer time.

▇ Study 2/Hannah: A Cry and a Song

Question 2. This ordinary story shows that no hurt is too personal or too trivial for God's attention. But this simple story also marks a turning point in Israel's history, from the dark era of the judges to the great era of the kings.

Question 3. Hannah's pain drove her to God. The vow she made in the midst of her pain resulted in a child who would be reared in the temple and who would later use that background to lead Israel through critical years in its history.

Question 6. It is significant to note that Hannah rejoiced in the *Lord,* not in the child.

Question 8. The term "seven sons" in 1 Samuel 2:5 refers to a number of completeness. Verse 21 tells the exact number of children Hannah eventually had.

Question 9. In 1 Samuel 2:10 Hannah's prayer is prophetic, "anticipating the establishment of kingship in Israel and the initial realization of the Messianic ideal in David (Luke 1:69). Ultimately her expectation finds fulfillment in Christ and his complete triumph over the enemies of God" *(The NIV Study Bible,* p. 377. Grand Rapids, Mich.: Zondervan, 1985).

Question 11. Prayer opened the way for God to work in Hannah's barrenness. Hannah didn't give up, but persisted in prayer. She carried through in the vow she made and worshiped God for his greatness.

■ Study 3/David: A Prayer at the End of Life

Question 1. Not all group members will have had positive models of giving. Encourage each person to share, learning from both positive and negative models.

Question 2. This background passage to David's prayer shows a number of principles for giving: The project was for God, not for people (1 Chronicles 29:1). David and the leaders set the example in giving (verses 2, 6). They consecrated themselves as well as their gifts (verse 5). They gave willingly, freely, and wholeheartedly (verse 9). They rejoiced as they gave (verse 9).

Question 8. Encourage group members to look at the whole passage to note things David and the people did, such as giving willingly and wholeheartedly (verse 6), rejoicing greatly (verse 9), praising the Lord (verse 10), praying (verses 10-19), bowing low and falling prostrate (verse 20), sacrificing offerings (verse 21), eating and drinking in the presence of God (verse 22).

■ Study 4/Solomon: "Hear and Forgive"

Question 3. By kneeling, Solomon showed he was submitting to a higher authority. He recognized God as the ultimate king and encouraged the people to do the same. By spreading his hands toward heaven, he was acknowledging that his help came from God.

Question 5. Solomon affirmed that not even the highest heaven could contain God, much less a temple. Yet God would be present in the temple in a special way.

Question 7. God is everywhere, so he did not live in the temple exclusively. But the temple was a visible symbol for the people of the invisible presence of God. He was specially present in the temple, though not limited by it.

Question 8. As you read this section, have a different person read each paragraph. This will add emphasis to the different situations described.

Question 9. Encourage group members to glance through all the verses in this section looking for the action words Solomon uses in reference to God. You will find many.

Question 13. Scan all of today's Scripture again, noticing the characteristics of God that Solomon refers to. Then encourage prayers of praise for characteristics such as his faithfulness, his promise-keeping, his forgiveness, his presence, his love, and his goodness.

◼ Study 5/Job: Trusting God for Who He Is

Question 5. The picture of God that emerges is powerful and majestic—yet he is also a God who wants to enter into a personal conversation with Job.

Question 7. Job says, "I put my hand over my mouth." This was a customary gesture of that time to show respect or to indicate that words were insufficient.

Question 13. Job was restored completely—materially, physically, and spiritually. One sign of his spiritual restoration was his intercessory prayer for his friends. As Job prayed for those who had wronged him, God blessed him.

◼ Study 6/Daniel: A Scriptural Agenda for Prayer

Question 2. "Daniel's prayer rose out of a tension between God's written truth and the world he saw around him. Most of us experience no such tension. The Word drifts over us as the world drifts by us" (*Daring to Draw Near,* p. 69).

Question 9. A helpful guide for using the Scriptures in prayer is *Pocket Prayers* by Robert C. Savage (Wheaton, Ill.: Tyndale, 1982).

Question 11. We seldom think of God's honor and reputation as important subjects for our prayers. A book that can help your group to pray for God's honor worldwide is *Operation World,* by Patrick Johnstone (William Carey Library, P.O. Box 111228-C, Pasadena,

CA 91104). It outlines specific needs in every country with suggestions for prayer.

Question 12. Encourage group members to tie together life needs and Scripture. As you pray, include the elements of confession, worship, and intercession that Daniel did.

Study 7/Habakkuk: Praying with God's Perspective

Question 2. These verses probably refer to God's mighty acts in delivering the people of Israel from Egypt (Exodus 14).

Question 8. In a farming economy, Habakkuk knew that crop failure and death of flocks would devastate the land. But even in the face of starvation, Habakkuk affirmed his joy in God.

Question 10. Encourage group members to name some of the fears they have for the future and to pray together about these, following Habakkuk's example.

Study 8/The Levites: A Prayer of Corporate Confession

Question 3. Encourage group members to note God at work in creation (Nehemiah 9:6), in the Abrahamic covenant (verses 7-8), in the exodus from Egypt (verses 9-11), in the desert wanderings (verses 12-21), in the conquest of Canaan (verses 22-25), and in the period of the judges (verses 26-28). The rest of the prayer speaks of God's work through the prophets (verses 26-31) and in their present situation (verses 32-37).

Question 4. After seventy years of captivity in Babylon, Israel was being restored as a nation. It was important to review in detail God's purposes for them as a nation. Because they had intermarried with foreigners, their special identity and mission were jeopardized, and they recognized the need to go back to their original calling.

Question 10. The theme of this prayer is God's faithfulness compared to humankind's failure, as summed up in verse 33. God's patience, mercy, and justice are highlighted through the prayer, along with the recognition of sin as the source of their great distress.

■ Study 9/Mary: A Prayer of Joy

Question 3. Notice the names of the child in Luke 1:31-32, 35 and his destiny in verse 33.

Question 4. Mary was fearful, yet believing. It seemed impossible for her to be with child since she was a virgin, but she submitted to God's unique plan for the Holy Spirit to come upon her so that the child would be the Son of God. She accepted the angel's words that "nothing is impossible with God."

Question 8. Mary expresses a joyful relationship with God. She recognizes that the holy God has dealt personally with her, and she worships him for this. It is obvious that Mary was very familiar with the Old Testament since her prayer is rooted in references to the Old Testament. Her beautiful response does not come out of a spiritual vacuum, but out of a close relationship to God. If you have time, compare Mary's prayer to Hannah's prayer in 1 Samuel 2:1-10.

■ Study 10/Jesus: A Prayer for His Family

Question 2. The essence of prayer is communication with God— not what is said, or where, or how. There is a place for public prayer, but our focus needs to be on *God* as the audience, not other people.

Question 4. Jesus taught this prayer to his followers, to people who had been forgiven their sins. It is the prayer of children to a Father who delights to meet their needs.

Question 5. It's interesting to think of the titles Jesus could have used instead of "Father"—"High and Mighty One," "Jehovah," or "All-powerful Creator." Jesus uses the intimate family word "Father," which is similar to our affectionate "Daddy."

Question 6. When Jesus says *our* Father, he links the disciples to himself and to each other in a family relationship.

Question 8. God's name stands for all he is—his character, nature, and actions. Hallowed means "treated as holy."

Question 11. This prayer covers present need (daily bread), past sin, and future trials. It deals with the spiritual, physical, and emotional dimensions of our lives.

Question 12. "Debts" has the same meaning as "sins." Jesus is not teaching that our forgiveness of others earns us the right to be forgiven. Instead he means that God forgives only the penitent, and a forgiving spirit is one of the evidences of true penitence.

◼ Study 11/Jesus: A Farewell Prayer

Question 2. Jesus wanted to be glorified so that he could in turn glorify the Father. Before Jesus came to earth, he was in a place of honor in heaven. Now that his mission on earth was almost completed, he asked to return to that exalted position at the right hand of God.

Question 6. From Jesus' prayer, we see the world as a battle-ground between the forces under Satan's power and those under

God's power. Jesus recognized the dangers of this hostile world, but did not ask for his disciples to be removed from it. Instead, he asked that they would be protected as they lived for God in the world.

Question 9. " . . . the unity is already given, not something to be achieved. The meaning is 'that they continually be one' rather than 'that they become one.' The unity is to be like that between the Father and the Son. It is much more than unity of organization . . ." *(The NIV Study Bible,* p. 1630).

■ Study 12/Paul: Bold Prayer for Ultimate Concerns

Question 2. Since the Ephesian believers are being built together to form God's household (Ephesians 2:19-22), Paul now prays that they will be rooted and established in deep faith and love.

Question 4. Paul says that all God's family members—Jewish or Gentile—have the right to call themselves his children because they have been adopted into his family.

Question 7. God's love is not unknowable, but it is so great that it cannot be completely known.

Question 8. Paul emphasizes that faith is not mere head knowledge. " . . . That Christ may dwell in your hearts through faith" was a prayer for Christ to be completely at home in their lives. Their faith would show itself in love and in power.

Question 11. Paul's petitions focus on the godly goals he longs to see in the lives of the believers. Now his doxology of praise focuses on the ultimate goal of existence—the glory and praise of God.

WHAT SHOULD WE STUDY NEXT?

To help your group answer that question, we've listed the Fisherman Guides by category so you can choose your next study.

TOPICAL STUDIES

Becoming Women of Purpose, Barton

Building Your House on the Lord, Brestin

Discipleship, Reapsome

Doing Justice, Showing Mercy, Wright

Encouraging Others, Johnson

Examining the Claims of Jesus, Brestin

Friendship, Brestin

The Fruit of the Spirit, Briscoe

Great Doctrines of the Bible, Board

Great Passages of the Bible, Plueddemann

Great People of the Bible, Plueddemann

Great Prayers of the Bible, Plueddemann

Growing Through Life's Challenges, Reapsome

Guidance & God's Will, Stark

Higher Ground, Brestin

How Should a Christian Live? (1,2, & 3 John), Brestin

Marriage, Stevens

Moneywise, Larsen

One Body, One Spirit, Larsen

The Parables of Jesus, Hunt

Prayer, Jones

The Prophets, Wright

Proverbs & Parables, Brestin

Relationships, Hunt

Satisfying Work, Stevens & Schoberg

Senior Saints, Reapsome

Sermon on the Mount, Hunt

The Ten Commandments, Briscoe

When Servants Suffer, Rhodes

Who Is Jesus? Van Reken

Worship, Sibley

BIBLE BOOK STUDIES

Genesis, Fromer & Keyes

Job, Klug

Psalms, Klug

Proverbs: Wisdom That Works, Wright

Ecclesiastes, Brestin

Jonah, Habakkuk, & Malachi, Fromer & Keyes

Matthew, Sibley

Mark, Christensen

Luke, Keyes

John: Living Word, Kuniholm

Acts 1-12, Christensen

Paul (Acts 13-28), Christensen

Romans: The Christian Story, Reapsome

1 Corinthians, Hummel

Strengthened to Serve (2 Corinthians), Plueddemann

Galatians, Titus & Philemon, Kuniholm

Ephesians, Baylis

Philippians, Klug

Colossians, Shaw

Letters to the Thessalonians, Fromer & Keyes

Letters to Timothy, Fromer & Keyes

Hebrews, Hunt

James, Christensen

1 & 2 Peter, Jude, Brestin

How Should a Christian Live? (1, 2 & 3 John), Brestin

Revelation, Hunt

BIBLE CHARACTER STUDIES

Ruth & Daniel, Stokes

David: Man after God's Own Heart, Castleman

Job, Klug

King David: Trusting God for a Lifetime, Castleman

Elijah, Castleman

Men Like Us, Heidebrecht & Scheuermann

Peter, Castleman

Paul (Acts 13-28), Christensen

Great People of the Bible, Plueddemann

Women Like Us, Barton

Women Who Achieved for God, Christensen

Women Who Believed God, Christensen